Original title:
Overcoming Together

Copyright © 2024 Swan Charm
All rights reserved.

Author: Swan Charm
ISBN HARDBACK: 978-9916-89-829-1
ISBN PAPERBACK: 978-9916-89-830-7
ISBN EBOOK: 978-9916-89-831-4

Through Shadows We Shine

In darkness we walk, hand in hand,
Guided by faith, where we stand.
Through trials we face, our spirits rise,
Together we soar, beyond the skies.

With whispers of light, our hearts ignite,
In shadows we trust, our souls in flight.
Each step we take, a sacred vow,
In the embrace of grace, we humble bow.

In Communion's Embrace

We gather as one, under His gaze,
In love's warm arms, our spirits blaze.
Breaking the bread, our hearts align,
In communion's grace, His light will shine.

With every prayer, a bond is made,
In unity's strength, we shall not fade.
The cup we share, a sacred sign,
In communion's joy, our souls entwine.

Forging a Path in Unity

Together we march, with purpose clear,
Each step we take, we banish fear.
In harmony's song, we find our way,
Joyful in trust, we greet the day.

For every heart, a thread we weave,
In kindness' warmth, we dare believe.
A tapestry rich, our spirits blend,
In unity's love, we shall transcend.

The Echoes of Our Hope

In silence we listen, to whispers near,
Echoes of hope, soft and clear.
Through trials and storms, we stand so tall,
Holding each other, we shall not fall.

With faith as our guide, the dawn will break,
Each dream alive, with every stake.
In the melodies sung, our spirits soar,
The echoes of hope, forevermore.

Steps in Faith

In shadows deep, we find the light,
With every step, our hearts take flight.
Trust in His plan, we rise above,
Guided by grace, surrounded by love.

Through trials faced, we stand as one,
In every battle, His will be done.
Climbing the mountains, our spirits soar,
In faith we walk, forevermore.

A Journey Arm in Arm

Together we walk, through storm and sun,
Hand in hand, our hearts beat as one.
With kindness spoken, and laughter shared,
In love's embrace, we find we're prepared.

Each step we take, the path reveals,
Lessons learned, and truth that heals.
Fellowship strong, in troubled times,
We sing our hopes, in joyful rhymes.

The Power of Our Prayers

Whispers rise, like incense sweet,
Hands uplifted, we feel His heat.
In quiet trust, we share our dreams,
The power of prayers flows like streams.

Boundless faith in each heart beats,
As every soul in His love meets.
Together we stand, our voices strong,
In unity found, we all belong.

United in Purpose

With hearts aligned, our mission clear,
In service to others, we draw near.
Each act of love, a shining spark,
Igniting hope within the dark.

Together we labor, with purpose true,
Building a world where kindness grew.
In unity's strength, we strive and bend,
As instruments of peace, we transcend.

A Journey Shared in Serenity

In the light of dawn we rise,
Hand in hand, souls entwined.
Guided by faith, soft and wise,
In harmony, we seek, we find.

Through valleys deep, and mountains high,
The path of love, we choose to tread.
With hearts aglow, we breathe the sky,
Each step we take, by grace we're led.

In silence shared, a sacred bond,
Whispers weave through the air so pure.
Together we stand, of this we're fond,
In trust and peace, we feel secure.

Our spirits soar, like eagles fly,
Beneath the heavens vast and bright.
In gratitude, we lift our sigh,
For every day renews our light.

As stars align in night's embrace,
We gather strength from one another.
In this journey, a holy space,
A testament of sister and brother.

Whispers of Unity

In quiet moments, hearts convene,
A symphony of souls at play.
The whispers of love, soft and keen,
Echoing through the night and day.

With humble steps, we seek the truth,
In each other's eyes, a sacred spark.
From childlike joy to elder's youth,
Together we light the path, through dark.

In circles drawn where spirits blend,
We find our strength, the bonds of grace.
With open arms, we learn to mend,
In unity, we seek our place.

Through trials faced, we rise anew,
A tapestry of love we weave.
With every thread, a vibrant hue,
In whispered hope, we believe.

As nature sings her ancient song,
We gather close, our voices raised.
In harmony, we feel we belong,
In whispers of faith, we are amazed.

Through the Storms We Stand

In trials fierce, we seek Your grace,
Our hearts uplifted in this place.
For every wave that crashes near,
We find our strength, Your voice we hear.

In shadows deep, Your light appears,
You calm our doubts, erase our fears.
Through every storm, we hold Your hand,
In faith we rise, together we stand.

Threads of Hope

In woven dreams, Your promise stays,
A tapestry of sacred ways.
With every breath, we weave anew,
The threads of hope, O Lord, in You.

Through darkest nights, our spirits soar,
A guiding light, forevermore.
Each strand a prayer, each knot a song,
In unity, we find where we belong.

When Spirits Align

When hearts ignite and time stands still,
The bonds of love fulfill Your will.
In whispered prayers, we find our path,
In joyous grace, escape the wrath.

United souls, we gather near,
In sacred peace, dispelling fear.
With every heartbeat, spirits chime,
In harmony, we share the rhyme.

Gathering Light

In dawn's embrace, we gather light,
Together shining, pure and bright.
With every star, a story told,
In faith, we step, our hearts so bold.

In sacred moments, love takes flight,
We rise as one, igniting night.
Transforming shadows, we will see,
The path of truth, forever free.

Weaving Joy from Grief

In shadows deep where sorrows lay,
A light will shine, a guiding ray.
Through tangled threads of pain and strife,
We weave together, share this life.

From ashes rise a seed of grace,
In broken hearts, love finds its place.
As tears blend with the morning dew,
We craft a tapestry, bold and true.

In every loss, a lesson found,
In every silence, love's sweet sound.
With every heartache, we shall find,
The strength to heal and leave behind.

Each moment deep, each sorrow pure,
In joy and grief, we will endure.
Through trials faced, we shall reclaim,
The joy that's birthed from all this pain.

Let grief give way to laughter's song,
In unity, we all belong.
With every thread, let's weave the bright,
A future forged in love's soft light.

When Together We Rise

Upon the wings of hope we soar,
With hearts united, we implore.
In spirit's dance, we find our way,
Together strong, come what may.

As candles lit in darkest night,
We gather strength, our souls ignite.
In harmony, we lift each other,
Sisters, brothers, hand in hand, a mother.

When storms may rage and doubts assail,
Together we will surely prevail.
In faith we stand, not one alone,
Each voice a part, a mighty tone.

The trials fierce, the path unclear,
Together we'll dispel the fear.
In all our dreams, we rise above,
A testament to grace and love.

With every step, the journey flows,
In every heart, the courage grows.
When together we lift our eyes,
The world transforms, as we arise.

Spirits Intertwined

In silence deep, our spirits meet,
A sacred bond, a rhythmic beat.
Entwined in faith, we find our might,
Together shining, purest light.

Through trials faced, and storms endured,\nOur hearts unite, our love assured.
In every breath, we share this grace,
A dance of souls in time and space.

From whispered prayers to shouts of joy,
Each spirit strong, no pain can cloy.
With every heartbeat, deeper still,
Connection grows, a shared goodwill.

In joyful laughter, sorrow's balm,
Together raised, we find the calm.
In shared belief, our spirits climb,
Intertwined in love, transcending time.

When shadows fall and doubts arise,
We hold each other, no goodbyes.
A tapestry of souls refined,
In every moment, spirits intertwined.

Collective Courage

In every heart, a spark ignites,
Amid the dark, we seek the lights.
Together strong, we face the storm,
In courage found, our spirits warm.

Hand in hand, we journey forth,
In every struggle, we find worth.
With voices raised, we stand as one,
Collective courage, battle won.

When hope seems lost, we hold the flame,
With echoes loud, we call each name.
In unity, our strength revealed,
Together, wounds and fears are healed.

Through trials shared, the burdens light,
In every tear, we find the fight.
No longer lone, we rise as kin,
Collective heart, the strength within.

With every step, a legacy,
In harmony, our destiny.
For when we stand, and not apart,
Collective courage, one beating heart.

Together We Ascend

In faith we gather, hand in hand,
Facing trials with a steadfast stand.
Together we rise, our spirits entwined,
In the warmth of love, true strength we find.

With each step forward, we shed our fears,
Unified in purpose, through laughter and tears.
Grace guides our path, as we journey along,
In the chorus of hope, we sing our song.

Mountains may tremble and valleys may weep,
But together we soar, our promise we keep.
With hearts like eagles, we take to the skies,
In the arms of the Spirit, our freedom lies.

Through shadows and light, we stride side by side,
In the tapestry woven, our faith is our guide.
Together we ascend, through trials we rise,
In the bond of our love, forever it ties.

The Light of Shared Resolve

In the darkness, a flicker burns bright,
A flame shared by souls, igniting the night.
Whispers of courage, echo loud and clear,
In the heart of the gathering, we banish all fear.

Hand in hand, we create a path,
With compassion and strength, we conquer the wrath.
Every struggle we face, no burden is ours,
Together we shine like the sun and the stars.

Moments of silence, where spirits unite,
In the warmth of our love, the world feels right.
For in every challenge, a lesson we find,
As we walk in the light, our hearts intertwined.

Through valleys of sorrow, we mend what is broken,
With faith as our anchor, and love as our token.
The light of shared resolve, a beacon to see,
Guiding us onward, forever we'll be.

Bonds Forged in Adversity

Through trials we walk, hand in hand,
In the crucible of life, we take a stand.
Our hearts, once separate, now beat as one,
Forged in the fire, our journey begun.

Each challenge we face, like iron to steel,
Strengthens the bonds, the love that we feel.
In the depths of despair, we find our way home,
Together, unyielding, we choose to roam.

When storms rage around us, we find inner peace,
In the embrace of the struggle, we find our release.
Through shadows we wander, yet light ever glows,
For the strength of our spirit in adversity shows.

With every tear shed, with every hard fall,
We rise even higher, united through all.
Bonds forged in adversity, treasures divine,
Guided by grace, in each heartbeat, we shine.

When Hearts Align

When hearts align, the world becomes whole,
In the union of spirits, we nourish the soul.
With kindness like rivers, our love freely flows,
Embracing each other, the warmth ever grows.

In the tapestry woven, our lives intertwine,
Through moments of laughter, through each quiet sign.
With empathy's power, we heal and restore,
In the light of our bond, we forever explore.

From shadows to sunlight, through valleys we roam,
In the circle of trust, we create a home.
With hearts beating gently, we dance through the day,
In the love that surrounds us, we'll never betray.

Together we journey, with faith as our guide,
In the beauty of living, we stand side by side.
When hearts align, the spirit takes flight,
In the harmony shared, we bask in the light.

Families of the Faithful

In the quiet dawn, we gather near,
Hearts intertwined, the message clear.
Together we rise, hand in hand,
Guided by love, united we stand.

Through trials and joy, our spirits share,
A bond so strong, beyond compare.
In faith we trust, as candles burn,
Each flicker a lesson, each moment we learn.

In prayer's embrace, we find our way,
To cherish each other, come what may.
With laughter and tears, we shape our role,
As families of faith, we nurture the soul.

Together we'll sing, through night and day,
With hearts ablaze, forever we'll stay.
In the warmth of grace, we find our might,
Families of the faithful, in love's pure light.

As seasons change, our roots run deep,
In the harvest of hope, we sow and reap.
Together we'll stand, through thick and thin,
In the arms of the sacred, we always begin.

Together Through the Storm

When shadows gather, we won't despair,
With hands held tight, we find our prayer.
In the howling winds, our spirits soar,
Together we seek what faith has in store.

Each raindrop whispers of trials to face,
Yet we march forth, in love and grace.
For within our hearts, a light remains,
An unyielding hope, through fear and pains.

With courage we forge, our journey's path,
In the eye of the storm, we feel love's wrath.
Together we shield, together we mend,
Our faith like a fortress, will never bend.

Though thunder roars, and darkness prevails,
In each other's strength, we find the trails.
As anchors of faith in turbulent seas,
Together we weather, with hearts at ease.

In every tempest, we rise anew,
A family of souls, steadfast and true.
Together through storms, we learn to believe,
In love's wild winds, together we cleave.

Kindred Spirits Ascending

Two souls entwined, in sacred flight,
Together we rise, to reach the light.
Bound by a love that transcends the earth,
In kindred spirits, we find our worth.

Through valleys low, and mountains high,
With hearts as one, we soar the sky.
In every prayer, in every song,
Together we whisper where we belong.

With wings of faith, we stretch and glide,
In unity's grace, we shall abide.
With every moment, our spirits dance,
In a divine embrace, we take our chance.

Through life's great trials, we stand as one,
In kindness' glow, the battles are won.
As stars above in the night's stole,
Guiding our way, they bless the soul.

Kindred spirits on paths we tread,
In love's warm light, no shadows spread.
Ascending together, we break each chain,
A journey of faith, profound and plain.

Lifting Each Other Higher

In each kind word, we plant the seed,
To lift each other, to nurture the need.
In shared laughter, and gentle grace,
Together we form a sacred space.

With hands outstretched, we share our load,
In kindness' embrace, we walk the road.
As beacons of hope, we shine so bright,
In love's warm glow, we find our light.

Through trials faced, we gather near,
In every setback, we quell the fear.
With hearts aligned, our spirits soar,
Guided by love, we seek to explore.

We rise together, no soul left behind,
In unity's strength, the lost we find.
Each act of love a step we take,
In lifting each other, new bonds we make.

As mountains tremble, we stand our ground,
In faith's embrace, our purpose found.
Lifting each other, forever we strive,
In love's grand mission, we feel alive.

Networked in Grace

In the web of souls we find,
A thread of love, pure and kind.
Each heart a beacon, shining bright,
Together we dance in sacred light.

Every prayer, a whisper shared,
In harmony, we are prepared.
Hand in hand, we rise and soar,
Embraced by grace forevermore.

With every heartbeat, we align,
A tapestry, truly divine.
Let faith connect our every part,
In this network, we will start.

Through trials faced with hope and trust,
In this bond, we are robust.
United voices, lifting high,
In grace, our spirits shall not die.

Together we weave the sacred song,
In love's embrace, we belong.
In every moment, rise and flow,
This network of grace will ever grow.

A Bridge of Hearts

Upon the river of life we stand,
With open arms, we lend a hand.
Building bridges, soul to soul,
In unity, we are made whole.

Love's gentle current flows between,
In every heart, a sacred dream.
Connecting us through every mile,
A bond that brings forth every smile.

Through storms that rage and winds that blow,
With faith, we face what we don't know.
Together we walk on this bridge,
With grace we conquer, we won't hedge.

Let kindness be our guiding star,
No matter where, no matter how far.
In each heart, the light we see,
This bridge of love will set us free.

In every heartbeat, we are thus,
A sacred path, in love we trust.
Together we'll rise, and never part,
Forever bound, a bridge of hearts.

Tides of Togetherness

In the ocean of life, we sway,
The tides of love guide our way.
Hand in hand, we rise and fall,
In togetherness, we hear the call.

Like waves that dance upon the shore,
We gather strength, we gather more.
With every swell, we find our place,
In the rhythm of divine embrace.

Through ebb and flow, we stand as one,
A sacred mission has begun.
With hearts entwined, we shall prevail,
In love's embrace, we cannot fail.

In unity, our spirits soar,
Each heartbeat echoes evermore.
In this ocean, vast and deep,
We sow the seeds of hope we keep.

Together we face the tides that come,
In harmony, our hearts are one.
With every wave, a promise made,
In this togetherness, we are laid.

The Sacred Convergence

In sacred spaces, we converge,
With open hearts, we feel the urge.
Together we rise, a vibrant whole,
In unity, we find our role.

With every breath, we seek the light,
In the darkness, we ignite the night.
A gathering of souls, divine,
In this convergence, love will shine.

Through trials faced, we stand as one,
Bound by the threads that love has spun.
In every journey, we shall share,
A tapestry beyond compare.

In the whispers of the sacred truth,
We find the wisdom of our youth.
Together we strive, hand in hand,
In this convergence, we understand.

With faith that binds, we shall be free,
In the sacred space, you and me.
Together we thrive, together we sing,
In love's embrace, we find our wings.

The Altar of Unity

At the altar of unity we gather,
Hands clasped in faith and grace.
Voices rise in joyful song,
Hearts aligned, we'll find our place.

In the light of truth we stand,
Together, though the path be long.
Each step taken, side by side,
Our journey blessed, our spirits strong.

Let not the world draw us apart,
For in each soul, a light shall gleam.
Through trials faced and burdens shared,
In unity, we weave our dream.

With open hearts, we lift our prayers,
A tapestry of hope and love.
Each thread connects, a sacred bond,
Guided by the hand above.

In harmony, we seek the peace,
A holy place where grace abides.
At the altar of unity we meet,
Together, casting aside our divides.

Drawing Strength from One Another

We walk this path, hand in hand,
In the beauty of fellowship's glow.
In trials faced, we find our strength,
Together, we rise and grow.

With every burden that we share,
The weight is lightened by our grace.
In each other's eyes, a spark ignites,
A radiant warmth, a safe embrace.

Voices mingle, dreams intertwine,
In the spirit of love, we thrive.
We gather courage from our hearts,
In unity, we're truly alive.

Let kindness be our guiding star,
In darkness, we illuminate the way.
With faith as our shield and guide,
We stand together, come what may.

Drawing strength from one another,
In every laugh and every tear.
Together we forge the path ahead,
In the light of love, we conquer fear.

Together Towards the Horizon

Together, we take the first step,
As dawn breaks with a golden ray.
With hope as our compass, we embark,
Towards the horizon, come what may.

In the warmth of friendship's embrace,
We navigate the winding road.
Each mile shared, a treasure found,
In love's reflection, we unload.

Through storms that may darken our skies,
We'll weather them, hand in hand.
With hearts ignited, undeterred,
In faith, our spirits will stand.

The horizon calls with a gentle voice,
Each promise brightens the path ahead.
Together in purpose, we shall rise,
With love as our eternal thread.

As we walk towards the horizon's end,
Let our hearts sing a sacred song.
In unity, forever bound,
Together is where we all belong.

Illuminated by Love

In the depths of night, love shines bright,
A guiding star when hope is thin.
With every heartbeat, a sacred light,
Illuminated by love, we begin.

In the whispers of the quiet dawn,
We find the strength to carry on.
With hands raised high, and spirits bold,
In love's embrace, we aren't alone.

Through trials fierce, our spirits soar,
When shadows loom, we stand as one.
In every story that we share,
Our journey blessed, the battle won.

Let love be the lantern we hold,
Lighting paths where darkness roams.
In every heart, a flame ignites,
Illuminated, we find our homes.

Together, we sing love's timeless song,
In every moment, let it flow.
For in this unity, we are strong,
Illuminated by love's bright glow.

On Wings of Grace

Upon the dawn, the light descends,
Filling our hearts with love that mends.
Casting aside our burdens and strife,
In every moment, we find new life.

The gentle whisper of sacred air,
Lifts our spirits, free from despair.
As we journey on this hallowed quest,
In faith and hope, we find our rest.

With wings of grace, the soul does soar,
Embracing each gift, forevermore.
United in spirit, we walk in peace,
In every blessing, our joys increase.

Let kindness be the song we sing,
For in such love, new paths will spring.
Together we rise, a radiant choir,
Igniting our hearts with holy fire.

In gratitude, we lift our praise,
For every dawn and golden haze.
With wings of grace, we come alive,
In this divine dance, we thrive.

A Tapestry of Hope

Threads of light weave through the night,
Creating a tapestry, pure and bright.
Each knot a story, every hue a prayer,
Intertwined destinies, woven with care.

In shadows cast, we find our grace,
Embracing each moment, we seek our place.
With every stitch, we mend the fray,
In unity, we hold the dark at bay.

Through trials faced, our spirits rise,
Guided by love, we reach for the skies.
Together we share each burdened sigh,
In this sacred bond, we'll never die.

The colors of kindness bathe our souls,
In this mosaic, our purpose unfolds.
As we journey forth, hand in hand,
A tapestry of hope across the land.

In every heart, a spark ignites,
Illuminating paths on starry nights.
In love's embrace, we weave our fate,
A symphony of dreams, forever great.

The Strength of Many Voices

In every whisper, a power grows,
Collective dreams where harmony flows.
Together we rise, our spirits entwined,
The strength of many, love redefined.

With each voice raised, a flame ignites,
Illuminating dark with shared insights.
Through trials faced, we stand as one,
Embracing each challenge, never undone.

From valleys deep to mountain high,
United we stand; no fear, no lie.
In songs of faith, our hope is clear,
The strength of many, forever near.

As echoes ring in the heart of time,
Each note a prayer, each word a rhyme.
In solidarity, we find the way,
Together we journey, come what may.

Through midnight's veil, our voices sing,
In unison, joy and peace we bring.
Bound by our love, we lift and rejoice,
Revealing the truth in the strength of voice.

In Harmony We Heal

In stillness found, our hearts align,
Whispers of peace, pure and divine.
As melodies blend, our souls connect,
In harmony's embrace, we gently reflect.

Through trials faced and wounds we bear,
Together we rise, united in care.
With every note, pain starts to fade,
In love's gentle flow, our hearts are remade.

The symphony of life, a sacred song,
In every chord, we all belong.
With open arms, we find our place,
In the rhythm of love, we seek grace.

Each heartbeat echoes, a sacred beat,
Binding our dreams, making us complete.
In the dance of compassion, we take a stand,
Hearts intertwined, hand in hand.

With every breath, we choose to heal,
In love's embrace, we truly feel.
Together we journey, spirits aligned,
In harmony, soul's purpose defined.

The Pathway of Many Feet

In the light of the dawning day,
Footsteps gather, hearts at play.
Together we walk, hand in hand,
Seeking joy in this blessed land.

Each step whispers stories untold,
Of faith and love, both brave and bold.
With every stride, we share our dreams,
Weaving hope within the seams.

Clouds may rise, storms may roar,
But our spirits will always soar.
In unity's bond, we find our song,
The path is long, but we are strong.

Mountains high, valleys low,
Through trials faced, together we grow.
In the warmth of our fellowship,
We discover true worship and kinship.

So let us walk, this sacred path,
With gratitude, we shun all wrath.
In diversities embrace, we see,
The strength of many, spirit set free.

Wisdom Born from Many

In diverse voices, wisdom sings,
Echoes of life, of ancient things.
Gathered around the sacred fire,
Each story shared lifts us higher.

From humble hearts, great truths arise,
The gift of knowledge beneath the skies.
In every tale, a lesson lies,
Bringing tears and joyful sighs.

We learn from mountains, rivers wide,
In each other, we take pride.
Through laughter, struggle, tears and grace,
Wisdom unfolds in every space.

Together we strive to understand,
With open minds and hearts so grand.
In unity's embrace, we find our way,
Guided by love, light from day.

So let us cherish each voice we hear,
For in our differences, the path is clear.
With minds and hearts forever learning,
Wisdom flourishes, bright and burning.

With Hearts as One

In the silence, our hearts combine,
In unison, our spirits shine.
Bound by love, in grace we stand,
Together, united, hand in hand.

With melodies rich, we elevate,
Each prayer spoken, we cultivate.
Harmony flows from every soul,
We're woven together, beautifully whole.

In the glow of the moon's embrace,
We seek solace in every face.
With gentle words, we mend the seams,
Crafting hope from our shared dreams.

As paths converge in sacred space,
We find purpose, we find grace.
With hearts aligned, we journey far,
Each moment treasured, a guiding star.

So let us rise, with strength anew,
In every heart, love's light shines through.
With hearts as one, we'll find our way,
Lighting the world, come what may.

Our Strength in Diversity

From many colors of the earth,
In every story lies great worth.
In diverse shades, our beauty glows,
A tapestry of life that grows.

Through varied paths, our spirits soar,
Understanding blooms, forevermore.
In every heart, a different beat,
Together we rise, never defeat.

Our strength resides in differences,
In shared laughter and experiences.
Embracing all, we find our truth,
The wisdom found in age and youth.

So let us gather, hand in hand,
Celebrate this vast, divine land.
For unity thrives in our embrace,
A cherished bond, a sacred space.

In diversity, our spirits blend,
With open hearts, we comprehend.
Together we'll weave a world so fair,
Our strength in diversity, beyond compare.

Strength in Our Embrace

In the quiet of the dawn, we rise,
Hearts entwined beneath the skies.
With every breath, we feel the grace,
In faith we find our sacred space.

Together we stand, hand in hand,
Bound by love, we understand.
Through trials fierce, we hold so tight,
Our spirits soar, our souls take flight.

In darkest nights, a light we share,
A whispered prayer, a tender care.
With every heartbeat, we ignite,
The strength of love, our guiding light.

Gentle whispers in the breeze,
Comfort found beneath the trees.
In unity, we find our way,
Our promise bright, come what may.

Embrace the storms that life may bring,
In every struggle, our hearts will sing.
For in this bond, we rise above,
Together, wrapped in endless love.

Faith's Gentle Embrace

In warmth of morning light, we dwell,
With trust that guides, our stories tell.
Each moment blessed, in sacred sight,
Faith's gentle touch brings purest light.

Through valleys low and mountains high,
We lift our gaze, to heaven's sky.
A tethered heart, in silence woven,
With every prayer, we're gently driven.

In whispers soft, the spirit speaks,
In every heart, the love we seek.
Through trials faced, our roots grow deep,
In faith's embrace, our souls shall keep.

As shadows fall and doubts arise,
We find our strength in unified ties.
In love's embrace, we cast away,
The burdens that would lead astray.

In hope's gentle arms, we find release,
A shining promise, a glimpse of peace.
With every step, in faith we trust,
Our hearts entwined, in God we must.

Bridging the Chasm

In a world divided, hearts in need,
Together, we plant the loving seed.
Across the void, our hands extend,
Building a path where spirits mend.

With every word, we sow the grace,
Creating bridges, a sacred space.
Inviting all to find their place,
In unity, we seek embrace.

As rivers swell, and storms do rage,
We gather strength, we turn the page.
In kindness shared and laughter bright,
We light the way with shared insight.

Each soul a story, each heart a song,
In every struggle, we all belong.
Together we stand, together we climb,
In bridging gaps, we transcend time.

With open arms, we forge the ties,
In love's reflection, the spirit flies.
For with each step, we heal the land,
In building dreams, together we stand.

The Path of Many

In the tapestry of life we weave,
Countless threads, each one believe.
With trails unknown, we walk our way,
In seeking light, both night and day.

Through winding paths and hidden doors,
In faith we walk to distant shores.
With courage bold, we face the tide,
Together on this sacred ride.

In moments lost, we find our voice,
In every choice, we make rejoice.
Through trials faced, we learn to grow,
As blessings come and teachings flow.

With every footstep, the journey shared,
In heart's embrace, we've all prepared.
For on this road, though different be,
We find our hope in unity.

With every sunrise painting the sky,
We lift our hearts, we learn to fly.
Embracing love, our spirits blend,
On this path of many, there's no end.

Together We Lift

In unity we stand, hearts entwined,
Together we lift, leaving fear behind.
Hands raised high, our spirits soar,
In this sacred bond, we are evermore.

Voices merge in harmony's song,
In each other's strength, we belong.
Faithful souls, we share the light,
Together we lift, banishing night.

With hope as our anchor, we sail forth,
In love's embrace, we find our worth.
One in purpose, hand in hand,
We rise together, a faithful band.

Mountains tremble, at our call,
In whatever storm, together we stand tall.
A tapestry woven, thread by thread,
In this divine union, we are fed.

Through trials faced, we find our way,
In love's embrace, we choose to stay.
Together we lift, as one we rise,
In this sacred journey, we touch the skies.

Love's Collective Strength

In love's embrace, we find our might,
A collective strength, shining bright.
Hearts interwoven, a sacred thread,
In every prayer, our spirits are fed.

Together we walk, on paths unknown,
With faith as our guide, we are never alone.
In storms of doubt, together we stand,
As one body, united, hand in hand.

When shadows whisper, we raise our voice,
In harmony's chorus, we rejoice.
Each moment shared, a treasure so rare,
In love's collective strength, we lay bare.

Through trials and triumphs, we remain,
Bound by a love that conquers all pain.
Together we shine, a beacon of trust,
In love's embrace, we always must.

In every heart, seeds of grace grow,
Together we flourish, making love flow.
With each gentle touch, we renew,
In love's collective strength, we are true.

The Faith that Unites

In quiet moments, our faith ignites,
Binding our souls with divine rights.
A gentle whisper, in the night,
The faith that unites, our guiding light.

Through valleys low and mountains steep,
In shared belief, our spirits leap.
With open hearts, we seek the truth,
In the faith that unites, we find our youth.

Together we gather, in sacred space,
Embracing each other, with love's grace.
In whispered prayers and dreams so bright,
The faith that unites, our endless flight.

A tapestry spun with threads so fine,
Each heart a story, divinely aligned.
In the faith that unites, we rise as one,
Together we'll shine, like the morning sun.

In trials faced and victories won,
That faith within us, forever runs.
With hope as our armor, we take our stand,
In the faith that unites, we live hand in hand.

In Spiritual Harmony

In stillness found, where spirits meet,
We dance in circles, hearts skip a beat.
In spiritual harmony, we thrive,
Together we sing, together we strive.

Each breath a prayer, a sacred sound,
In the depths of love, we are profound.
With hands held tight, we rise above,
In spiritual harmony, we find our love.

Our voices blend, a symphony,
Resonating through eternity.
With each soulful note, we rise and soar,
In spiritual harmony, forevermore.

In the calm of night, the dawning day,
Together we journey, lighting the way.
In faith's embrace, we stand as one,
In spiritual harmony, our work's begun.

Through valleys low and skies of blue,
In spiritual harmony, we renew.
With hearts aligned, we walk this place,
In love and faith, we find our grace.

Sacred Bonds of Resilience

In trials we find our strength anew,
Through faith and grace, the light breaks through.
With hands held high, we rise and stand,
Together we forge a sacred band.

Through storms that shake and winds that howl,
Our hearts unite, our spirits grow.
In every challenge, God's hand we trace,
Finding solace in His embrace.

When shadows loom and doubts arise,
We turn our gaze toward the skies.
In whispered prayers, we find our voice,
In sacred bonds, we make our choice.

With courage deep and hope ablaze,
We walk together through the haze.
In every step, the truth we seek,
In love's warm light, we are not weak.

Together we bind, with threads divine,
Resilience found in hearts that shine.
In unity, our spirits soar,
With sacred bonds, we are much more.

Voices in the Wilderness

In quiet woods, where echoes play,
Our whispered thoughts drift far away.
Each rustling leaf, each gentle hum,
  Reminds us of the love to come.

From mountaintops to valleys low,
The voice of God begins to flow.
In every breeze, a message clear,
  In wilderness, He draws us near.

With open hearts and humble minds,
We seek the truth that love unbinds.
In solitude, we hear the call,
  In every rise, we shall not fall.

Through trials vast, we tread the path,
In humble praise, we find His wrath.
For in the wild, the soul is free,
  To dance and sing in harmony.

Voices blend in sacred song,
In wilderness, we all belong.
With faith as guide, our hearts unite,
  In sacred ground, we find our light.

The Shield of Fellowship

In unity, we stand as one,
Beneath the rays of the morning sun.
With open arms and hearts so wide,
In fellowship, we shall abide.

When trials come, we shield each other,
With love and grace, like sister and brother.
In every storm, our spirits blend,
With every struggle, we shall mend.

Each laughter shared, each tear we cry,
A testament that we rely
On bonds that strengthen as we grow,
In fellowship, His love will flow.

With courage bright and visions clear,
We journey on, casting out fear.
Through trials fierce, we will not break,
In every heart, a vow we make.

Together we rise, with voices strong,
In the shield of fellowship, we belong.
With faith our guide and love our way,
In every step, we choose to stay.

Angels Beside Us

In moments dark, when hope seems lost,
We find our strength, whatever the cost.
For angels dwell in shadows deep,
Guarding promises that we keep.

With wings of light, they guide our way,
In whispered prayers, they help us stay.
Through trials faced and burdens shared,
In faith and love, we are prepared.

They walk beside us, hand in hand,
In every tear, they understand.
With gentle grace, they lift us high,
In every moment, they're nearby.

In laughter's joy and sorrow's night,
Their presence fills our hearts with light.
For in our journey, we are blessed,
With angels near, we find our rest.

So let us rise, with spirits free,
Embraced by love and harmony.
For angels beside us, always near,
In every heart, there's no need for fear.

A Journey of Sacred Hands

With hands uplifted, we seek the grace,
In quiet whispers, we find our place.
Each step adorned by faith's embrace,
Together we walk in this sacred space.

Our hearts ignited, a flame divine,
In unity's bond, our spirits entwine.
Through trials and shadows, in love we shine,
For every moment, God's light is mine.

Through the valleys, we climb and tread,
With sacred dreams that guide our thread.
In joy and sorrow, the path we spread,
With every heartbeat, His love is fed.

Hand in hand, we rise above,
In silent songs, we speak of love.
With sacred hands, we push and shove,
Together we are, in grace we move.

With every prayer, we heal and mend,
In faith's embrace, we learn to bend.
A journey blessed that will not end,
In sacred hands, we find our friend.

Love's Resounding Call

In gentle waves, the heart does swell,
A voice of hope, a sacred bell.
Through storms of doubt, we rise and dwell,
In love's embrace, all is made well.

Echoes of kindness, soft and clear,
In every whisper, we draw near.
With open hearts, we cast out fear,
For love's resounding call we hold dear.

Together we stand, in faith we grow,
With every seed of grace we sow.
In nurturing light, our spirits glow,
In love's resounding call, we know.

As rivers flow, so does His grace,
In every heart, we find our place.
With love extended, we run the race,
In harmony's song, we embrace.

Through trials faced, and burdens shared,
In unity's strength, our hearts are bared.
A tapestry of hope declared,
In love's resounding call, we are cared.

Glimmers of Shared Light

In twilight's grace, a spark ignites,
Amongst the shadows, hope ignites.
With every heart, a beacon bright,
In glimmers shared, we find our might.

With tender hands, we lift the soul,
In whispered dreams, we become whole.
Together united, we seek the goal,
In glimmers of light, we find our role.

Through tangled paths, we find our way,
In every dawn, a brand-new day.
With hearts aligned, together we sway,
In glimmers of shared light, we pray.

In every struggle, we rise anew,
With faith as armor, we will break through.
In friendship's warmth, our spirits grew,
In glimmers of shared light, we pursue.

For every story, a thread we weave,
In sacred trust, we dare believe.
In shared moments, we choose to cleave,
In glimmers of light, we shall achieve.

The Chorus of Resilience

In trials faced, we sing our song,
A chorus loud, where we belong.
With every heartbeat, we grow strong,
In resilience, we cannot go wrong.

Through darkest nights, we find the dawn,
In every struggle, we carry on.
With voices raised, we greet the morn,
In the chorus of life, we are reborn.

With love as our shield, we stand as one,
In every challenge, we are undone.
Together we rise, together we run,
In the chorus of resilience, we've won.

With each note sung, a bond is formed,
In unity's heart, we are warmed.
With joyful spirits that cannot be stormed,
In the chorus of hope, we are transformed.

For every laughter, a tear we share,
In the depths of love, we find our care.
With courage strong, we lay our bare,
In the chorus of resilience, we are rare.

A Tapestry of Belief

In faith we weave our souls so bright,
With threads of hope, we find the light.
Each prayer a stitch, each tear a thread,
Bound together where angels tread.

In shadows cast by doubt and fear,
Our hearts unite and persevere.
For in the hands of love, we stand,
Creating peace across the land.

Embrace the grace that comes our way,
In every sunset, every day.
We find our strength through trials faced,
A tapestry of love embraced.

As moments pass, our spirits rise,
With faith our guide, we seek the skies.
In every heart, a story sings,
Where hope resides, the joy it brings.

Together we are one and free,
In harmony, our souls agree.
A legacy of faith adorned,
A tapestry of love reborn.

Harmonized Souls

In quiet moments, souls align,
A gentle rhythm, love divine.
With every heartbeat, spirit speaks,
Uniting voices, strong yet meek.

Through trials faced and joys bestowed,
We walk together, love our road.
In every glance, a story shared,
Two hearts entwined, eternally paired.

The blessings flow like rivers wide,
In faith we trust, in hope we bide.
As day turns to night, still we sing,
Harmonized souls, eternal spring.

In prayers whispered to the skies,
We find the truth that never lies.
Our spirits soar on wings of grace,
In every challenge, love's embrace.

Together we rise, together we mend,
In love we trust, on faith depend.
Harmonized souls in every dance,
A symphony of life's sweet chance.

The Refuge of Togetherness

In crowded streets, we find our place,
A refuge built on love and grace.
In shared moments, joy unfolds,
Together etched in tales retold.

With open arms, we gather near,
In laughter shared, we cast out fear.
For in this circle, hearts reside,
The bond of faith, our faithful guide.

When shadows loom, and storms arise,
We seek the warmth in trusting eyes.
A refuge found in unity,
Together strong, we choose to be.

In whispered prayers, we hold the light,
With faith as armor, hearts take flight.
In every trial, love's gentle grace,
A refuge forged in time and space.

Though paths may wind, and mountains loom,
Together we thrive, dispelling gloom.
In every heartbeat, love's decree,
The refuge of togetherness, we see.

Guided by the Divine Light

In darkest hours, a lantern glows,
A beacon bright where love bestows.
With every step, we find our way,
Guided by the light of day.

In gentle whispers, hope returns,
For every heart, the spirit yearns.
As stars align in velvet skies,
We seek the truth that never dies.

Let faith be strong, let doubts disperse,
In trust we walk, the universe.
With open hearts, we rise each morn,
In gratitude, our souls reborn.

The light of kindness, pure and bright,
Illuminates the path of right.
In every choice, let love take flight,
Guided by the divine light.

Through trials faced and dreams pursued,
In every heart, a love renewed.
Together we shine, our spirits bright,
United as one in endless light.

Bridges of Faith

Across the waters wide we tread,
With hearts aglow, the path we spread.
Each step we take, a prayer, a song,
In unity, we all belong.

O'er valleys deep, on mountains high,
Our spirits soar, we touch the sky.
With every bridge we choose to build,
A testament of love fulfilled.

Through storms and trials, hand in hand,
Together strong, we make our stand.
In darkest nights, our candles shine,
Guiding souls, your light is mine.

From whispered hopes to shouts of glee,
A chorus rises, wild and free.
With faith our guide, we cannot fail,
Together, love will prevail.

In every heart, a spark ignites,
A flame that grows with shared delights.
Bridges of faith, strong and wide,
In God's embrace, we will abide.

The Mosaic of Strength

In every shard, a story lies,
Reflecting light from countless skies.
Together we form a boundless frame,
Each piece unique, yet one in name.

The colors blend in harmony,
Creating paths for all to see.
From trials faced, we rise anew,
With courage forged, our spirits true.

Each voice a note in sacred song,
In unity, we all belong.
For when we gather, hearts entwined,
A tapestry of love defined.

In shadows cast, we find our grace,
Through every tear, we find our place.
The mosaic gleams in life's embrace,
A testament of strength and faith.

So let us stand, though tempests roar,
Together strong, forevermore.
In every challenge, hope shall shine,
As we create this life divine.

Together We Rise

Together we rise on wings of prayer,
Through trials faced, we will not wear.
In every heartbeat, a sacred dance,
With faith as our shield, we take the chance.

With hands united, we journey forth,
In shared belief, we find our worth.
For every struggle, together we fight,
In the darkest hour, we share the light.

Embracing love, we find our might,
In every soul, a spark ignites.
Through valleys low and mountains steep,
In God's embrace, our dreams we keep.

With voices raised in sweet refrain,
We sing of hope amidst the pain.
Together we lift, together we build,
A sanctuary of hearts fulfilled.

So let us rise, let courage soar,
In every challenge, we'll love more.
With faith's embrace, we journey wide,
Together we rise; we shall abide.

Serenity in Our Union

In quiet moments, hearts align,
A gentle peace, a love divine.
Through trials faced, we find our way,
In serenity, we choose to stay.

With every whisper, softly shared,
A bond of trust, forever bared.
In unity, our spirits soar,
Together always, to explore.

Through stormy seas and sunlit skies,
In every tear, a chance to rise.
For in our hearts, we hold the key,
To endless love and harmony.

With grateful hearts, we walk this path,
In every joy, we feel the bath.
United strong, we shine so bright,
Our love, a beacon in the night.

So let us cherish this sacred bond,
In every heartbeat, we respond.
With serenity, our souls entwined,
In love's embrace, true peace we find.

The Power of Our Prayers

In whispers soft, we call Your name,
Hearts uplifted, we seek the same.
With fervent hopes, our voices blend,
In faith united, our spirits mend.

In shadows deep, Your light will shine,
Guiding us close, Your grace divine.
Each prayer a thread, from soul to sky,
Through every struggle, we learn to fly.

From aching hearts, we raise our pleas,
O Lord of mercy, bring us ease.
In every tear, a story shared,
In every prayer, our souls are bared.

Together we stand, hand in hand,
In hope we find, together we stand.
For love is power, love is grace,
With prayer's shield, we find our place.

So let us pray, with voices high,
In the sacred space, we lift the cry.
A symphony of faith unknown,
In the heart of prayer, we're never alone.

Jointly We Soar

On wings of love, together we rise,
Through trials and storms, beneath the skies.
With every step, hand in hand we'll go,
In unity strong, our spirits glow.

In harmony's song, our hearts unite,
Guided by truth, we shine so bright.
With fervent faith, we chase the dream,
In the light of hope, we form the beam.

Each voice a note, in the sacred choir,
Together forging, a path of fire.
With open hearts, and gentle grace,
We journey forth, in love's embrace.

As mountains bow, and valleys swell,
In Your embrace, we find our well.
Jointly we soar, on wings unseen,
In strength of numbers, forever keen.

So let us rise, O kindred friend,
In unity strong, this journey we'll tend.
With faith our guide, we reach for more,
Together in love, we jointly soar.

Crowned in Compassion

In gentle hands, we plant the seeds,
Of love and care, fulfilling needs.
A crown of grace, we humbly wear,
In acts of kindness, we show we care.

Through every tear, and every smile,
We walk together, each precious mile.
For every soul, a story unfolds,
In compassion's hold, our hearts behold.

Let mercy flow, like rivers wide,
In giving hearts, we find our pride.
With open arms, we share the load,
In helping hands, our love bestowed.

Each little deed, a beacon bright,
In darkest times, we become the light.
Crowned in compassion, we take our stand,
With hearts united, we lend a hand.

So let us rise, with love to share,
In every corner, show that we care.
Together we flourish, together we grow,
In a world of compassion, love will glow.

The Dawn After Dusk

In silent nights, when shadows creep,
We hold our dreams, our hopes we keep.
Yet with each dawn, the light will break,
A promise new, a path to take.

Though trials come, and fears may stir,
In morning's glow, our hearts confer.
A brand new day, the sun will rise,
With every breath, we touch the skies.

Through storms we've faced, and battles fought,
In faith and love, all lessons taught.
For after dusk, the light will show,
The beauty found in seeds we sow.

So as we walk, with courage bright,
The dawn will always follow night.
In every heart, a spark remains,
In hope's embrace, love never wanes.

We'll cherish moments, both dark and light,
Through every trial, we'll find our sight.
For in the dawn, our spirits sing,
A new beginning, hope takes wing.

When Grace Unfolds

In the quiet dawn, grace appears,
Gentle whispers, calming fears.
With open hearts, we seek the light,
Embracing peace, dispelling night.

Each step we take, a soft embrace,
In every moment, find His grace.
Like rivers flow, love intertwines,
In sacred stillness, spirit shines.

With every breath, a prayer we sing,
To the heavens, our voices bring.
In trials faced, we find our way,
Through faith renewed, we rise and sway.

Heaven's promise, forever true,
In every heart, He makes it new.
Together we stand, never alone,
In the garden of love, we've grown.

When grace unfolds, our souls align,
A tapestry of love divine.
In His embrace, we find our role,
As one in spirit, whole and whole.

The Unbreakable Circle

In light and shadow, we gather as one,
A circle unbroken, under the sun.
Hand in hand, in faith we abide,
With hearts as vessels, love's gentle tide.

Bound by the spirit, we rise and flow,
In unity's dance, our strength will grow.
Each soul a star, in heaven's own chart,
Together we shine, never apart.

With prayers lifted high, our voices soar,
In rhythm of life, we seek evermore.
Through trials and storms, we hold our ground,
In sacred connection, true peace is found.

Reflecting the light of His endless care,
In community's embrace, we are rare.
A circle of love, unbroken, we stand,
With faith as our guide, forever hand in hand.

As time goes by, our bond will ignite,
In the depths of love, we find our light.
Teaching each other, hearts intertwined,
In the unbreakable circle, grace defined.

In the Shade of Love

Beneath the branches, where shadows play,
We find our refuge, peace held at bay.
In the shade of love, our spirits sing,
A gentle breeze, the hope it brings.

With faithful hearts, we gather round,
In laughter shared, our joy is found.
Each tender moment, a gift we share,
Love's warm embrace, a balm, a prayer.

Through trials faced, we stand as one,
In the shade of love, battles are won.
With open arms, we welcome the day,
In unity's grace, we choose to stay.

The light within us, forever bright,
Guides us onward through the darkest night.
With every heartbeat, love whispers low,
In the shade of love, we learn to grow.

Together united, we'll rise above,
Crafting our story, a tale of love.
In life's embrace, find strength anew,
In the shade of love, His promise is true.

Voices as One

In the chorus of life, our voices blend,
A symphony skilled, on truth we depend.
With hearts attuned, we lift up the song,
In harmony's grace, we all belong.

From mountain high to valley low,
Each note a story, together we grow.
In silence shared, our spirits soar,
In joyous refrain, we seek the core.

With every word, a thread of gold,
Binding us closer, as we unfold.
In every heartbeat, a promise made,
In the light of love, no fear will cascade.

Voices united, we break all chains,
In the warmth of truth, our freedom reigns.
In times of sorrow, we stand as one,
A testament strong, our race is run.

By faith we stand, together we rise,
In the spirit of hope, boundless skies.
With voices as one, forever aware,
In the symphony of life, we declare.

The Journey of Many

In paths untread, we seek the light,
With hearts entwined, we rise in flight.
Through valleys deep, and mountains tall,
Together we journey, answering the call.

With faith as our guide, we press ahead,
Through trials and tribulations, we are led.
For in each step, our souls align,
United in purpose, your hand in mine.

The stars above, a guiding grace,
Reflect our dreams in endless space.
With every breath, our spirits sing,
In the journey of many, love is the king.

Through shadows dark, we stand as one,
Embracing hope till the day is done.
The journey's path may twist and bend,
Yet with each other, we find the end.

With every heartbeat, a tale we weave,
In togetherness, we dare to believe.
In the journey of many, we rise anew,
Together, forever, in all we pursue.

Together in the Refuge

In the shelter of love, we gather near,
Embracing the warmth, casting out fear.
With open hearts, we find our home,
Together in the refuge, never alone.

Through the storms of life, our spirits survive,
Within this haven, our hopes revive.
Hand in hand, we face the night,
Together in the refuge, we find the light.

With prayers ascended, our voices rise,
In harmony, we echo the skies.
The strength of many, as one, we stand,
Building a fortress, hand in hand.

In silence we speak, in love we trust,
Together we flourish, unite we must.
This bond is sacred, a treasure divine,
Forever in the refuge, our souls entwine.

With every heartbeat, this refuge blooms,
A haven of peace where kindness looms.
Together in the refuge, hearts aligned,
In the name of love, our spirits combined.

One Heart, One Spirit

In the quiet whispers of the night,
We share a dream, a radiant light.
One heart beats true, in shadows strong,
One spirit dances, where we belong.

Across the valleys, our courage shines,
Bound by the thread of sacred designs.
Together we rise, in faith we stand,
One heart, one spirit, hand in hand.

With every tear, our strength renews,
In every smile, the hope we choose.
Together we gather, under the sun,
One heart, one spirit, we are one.

Through trials faced, our bond secures,
With every challenge, love endures.
In the tapestry woven, our dreams align,
One heart, one spirit, perfectly divine.

As dawn breaks forth, we greet the day,
With gratitude shared in every way.
United in purpose, forever we'll be,
One heart, one spirit, eternally free.

From Many, One Song

In the symphony of life, we find our tune,
Different notes, yet we harmonize soon.
From many, one song, our voices blend,
Together we rise, together we mend.

With diverse melodies, our stories unfold,
In unity's chorus, a treasure untold.
Every heartbeat offers a unique refrain,
From many, one song, joy mingles with pain.

Through trials we face, the echoes remain,
Resilience in rhythm, love in the strain.
Let different voices resound with pride,
From many, one song, we stand side by side.

With every note, we strengthen the bond,
In the choir of life, we all respond.
Together we sing, in freedom we thrive,
From many, one song, we come alive.

As the final chord resonates through the night,
We find our peace in the shared delight.
From many, one song, a testament bold,
In the heart of the union, love will unfold.

When We Stand as One

In faith we gather, hands held tight,
Together we rise, embraced by light.
Our voices blend in sacred song,
In unity's strength, we all belong.

With hearts together, in joy we stand,
Guided by His most holy hand.
Each spirit shines, a radiant glow,
Together in love, we surely grow.

When trials come, we face the test,
Support as one, we find our rest.
Through darkest nights, our hope remains,
In shared belief, we break the chains.

Let kindness flow, like rivers wide,
With love's embrace, there's naught to hide.
When we stand as one, we are made whole,
In every heart, a sacred role.

So let us march, in peace we tread,
With every step, our spirits fed.
In harmony's grace, we draw near,
United in faith, we shall not fear.

United in Purpose

In humble hearts, our purpose shines,
With faith as strong as ancient pines.
Together we strive, with eyes on high,
In every prayer, our spirits fly.

Bound by the call of love divine,
In shared belief, our paths align.
With open hands, we serve and give,
Through acts of grace, we learn to live.

United in purpose, we rise as one,
In every struggle, we will not run.
With courage bold, we face the storm,
In sacred light, we are reborn.

Through trials faced, we find our voice,
In shared devotion, we rejoice.
Together we journey, hearts entwined,
In love's embrace, the lost we find.

With every step, our mission clear,
In faith we stand, casting out fear.
Let friendship bloom, let kindness reign,
United in purpose, we break the chain.

Journeys of the Heart

Each path we walk is ours to share,
With open hearts, we show we care.
In whispers soft, our dreams take flight,
With faith as wings, we chase the light.

Through valleys low and mountains high,
In every tear, a hope will sigh.
With courage found in every plea,
Our journeys lead to unity.

In friendships forged through joy and pain,
Together, we shall rise again.
With love as guide, we brave the road,
In every heart, His love bestowed.

Through every twist, each turn we take,
We hold each other when we break.
In strength we find, no task too great,
Together, love will navigate.

With open hearts, we venture forth,
In every soul, a sacred worth.
Through journeys shared, our spirits gleam,
In faith, we strive, we live the dream.

Guided by a Common Light

In twilight's glow, we seek the way,
With hearts alight, we greet the day.
Together we travel, hand in hand,
In shining grace, we take our stand.

With every step, our vision clear,
In love's embrace, we have no fear.
Through shadows cast, we find our path,
In every moment, we feel His wrath.

Guided by light, we stand as one,
In every struggle, we will not run.
Through trials faced, we grow in faith,
In every heart, His love lays grace.

United in spirit, we rise and sing,
In harmony's echo, our voices ring.
With eyes uplifted, we chase the sky,
In unity's bond, we will not die.

With hearts ablaze, let kindness lead,
In every thought, plant love's sweet seed.
Guided by light, forever true,
In every life, His love renews.

Through Trials We Blossom

In shadows deep, our hearts arise,
With faith as light, we reach the skies.
Through every storm, we learn to stand,
In trials faced, God holds our hand.

Each tear we shed, a seed will grow,
In prayer, His grace begins to flow.
From broken paths, the flowers bloom,
In darkest nights, His love consumes.

When burdens weigh, we rise anew,
With hope entwined, our spirits flew.
In wilderness, we find our song,
Through pain and grief, we still belong.

Our trials forge a strength so rare,
In unity, we find Him there.
Resilience grows, as faith ignites,
Through trials faced, we find the light.

With every step, we walk in grace,
In troubled times, we see His face.
Through trials bold, we take our flight,
In His embrace, we find our might.

Love's Collective Embrace

In love's sweet bond, we share our grace,
With open hearts, we find our place.
In kindness shown, our spirits blend,
Through every moment, we transcend.

Together strong, we lift our song,
In harmony, we all belong.
A circle formed, where hearts align,
In every hug, His love divine.

Through trials faced, we never part,
In shared belief, we heal the heart.
With gentle hands, we heal the pain,
In love's embrace, our hope remains.

We gather close, with voices raised,
In gratitude, our souls amazed.
Each story told, a thread of light,
In love's warm glow, we shine so bright.

With every smile, we spread the grace,
In every tear, a warm embrace.
Together, we shall face the storm,
In love's sweet bond, all hearts transform.

United We Pray

In quiet moments, we align,
With fervent hearts, our spirits shine.
In whispered prayers, we seek the way,
Together strong, united we pray.

Through trials shared, our faith holds fast,
In every plea, His love is cast.
With lifted hands, we touch the skies,
In every heart, His presence lies.

As one body, we find our strength,
In shared devotion, we go the length.
In unity, we rise and stand,
With faith unyielding, hand in hand.

When shadows loom, we call His name,
In fellowship, we fan the flame.
Through every dawn, our souls awake,
Together bold, His path we take.

In sacred space, our voices blend,
In hope alive, our spirits mend.
With every prayer, a chance to grow,
In unity, we let love flow.

The Gift of Fellowship

In circles drawn, we share our hearts,
With laughter bright, each moment starts.
In every smile, the ties enhance,
Through fellowship, we find our chance.

Together here, we lift our voice,
In sweetest harmony, we rejoice.
In love's embrace, we find our home,
With every step, we're not alone.

Through trials faced, we stand as one,
In shared belief, our battles won.
With open arms, we greet the dawn,
In fellowship, our fears are gone.

As seasons change, our bonds grow strong,
In moments shared, we all belong.
With prayerful hearts, we seek the light,
In fellowship, our souls take flight.

With every tear, we share the load,
In acts of love, our spirits flowed.
In this embrace, we find our bliss,
The gift of fellowship, pure love's kiss.

Harmony Forged Through Trials

In the furnace of strife, we rise,
Purified by flames, we find our ties.
Each challenge a stone in our shared path,
Together we dance in love's warm bath.

Through valleys of shadow, we walk aligned,
With hearts intertwined, our spirits unconfined.
The storms may rage, yet our faith stands strong,
In unity, we sing our sacred song.

In whispers of hope, our souls interlace,
Finding strength in the trials we face.
Let the journey shape us, a tapestry spun,
In the light of grace, we become as one.

With each tear that falls, we water the ground,
From ashes of sorrow, our dreams are found.
In the warmth of our love, we boldly ignite,
A beacon of peace, shimmering bright.

So let us stand firm, hand in hand we create,
A harmony born from a bond of fate.
In the fabric of life, our spirits entwined,
Through trials, together, our hearts are aligned.

Threads of Faith Interwoven

Each thread of belief, in colors so bright,
Stitched through the fabric, our faith takes flight.
Woven together, each story unfolds,
In the tapestry rich, our spirits are bold.

Through the silence of doubt, a whisper does flow,
Guiding our hearts with a radiant glow.
In the loom of existence, our dreams intertwine,
Fashioned by trials, our souls brightly shine.

With every stitch made in compassion's name,
The threads of our journeys ignite the same flame.
In shared understanding, our love finds its place,
A beautiful pattern, our divine embrace.

As we gather the pieces of life's sweet refrain,
Casting aside all the shadows of pain.
In the warmth of connection, we rise above strife,
These threads of our faith weave the fabric of life.

In moments of struggle, we hold each other near,
Embracing the weight of our joy and our fear.
For within this design, there's a lesson we find,
The threads of togetherness leave none behind.

Guided by Stars of Compassion

In the night so deep, our hearts look up high,
Finding stars of kindness that light up the sky.
Each twinkling light, a promise of grace,
Guiding our journey, we remember our place.

Through the darkness of doubt, these stars shall remain,
A beacon of love in the midst of our pain.
With each spark of hope, we rise hand in hand,
In the universe's embrace, together we stand.

Compassion, our compass, unwavering and true,
In the tapestry woven, it threads me and you.
Through the trials we face, their glow shall inspire,
The fire of our spirits, forever afire.

As we wander this path, with hearts open wide,
Chasing dreams under the night sky's tide.
With wisdom from stars, we make our way clear,
In the journey of love, we shed every fear.

So let us be guided by these celestial lights,
In the depths of our souls, we'll soar to new heights.
For in each act of compassion, we find our best dreams,
As stars lead us onward, so bright are our beams.

Sheltered by Sacred Bonds

In the garden of life, where love freely grows,
We find safety in bonds that the heart truly knows.
Each friendship a shelter, a fortress divine,
In the warmth of our presence, our spirits align.

Through storms of existence, together we stand,
With hands interlocked, we weather the land.
In whispers of trust, our hearts find release,
In the embrace of each other, we discover our peace.

With roots intertwined, we nurture our souls,
A family of faith, filling each other's roles.
Through trials we face, our shadows grow small,
In the light of our love, we're united through all.

As seasons keep changing, our bonds ever grow,
Together we flourish, in love we bestow.
Each moment a treasure, each promise a song,
In this sacred connection, we always belong.

So let us remain, forever entwined,
For in these sacred bonds, our hearts are aligned.
In the sanctuary built by compassion and care,
We're sheltered together, in the love that we share.

The Strength of Many Hearts

In unity we gather, hand in hand,
Our spirits soar high, a sacred band.
With faith as our guide, we shall not fall,
Together we rise, responding to the call.

Voices raised in harmony, a chorus divine,
Each heartbeat echoes, a promise to shine.
In struggles we find, our strength is revealed,
With love as our armor, our wounds are healed.

Across the valleys, in valleys so wide,
A tapestry woven, where grace does abide.
For every tear shed, new joy will arise,
The strength of many hearts reaches the skies.

Together we stand, in each other we trust,
Through trials and storms, our spirits adjust.
With every shared moment, we flourish and grow,
In the strength of many, our love will glow.

From darkness to dawn, we travel as one,
Together we'll shine, like the morning sun.
In the promise of hope, our destinies sync,
With the strength of many hearts, we shall not sink.

Together We Ascend

In the arms of the divine, we find our way,
With every step forward, we choose to stay.
Bound by the spirit, igniting the fire,
Together we ascend, our souls lifting higher.

With faith as our compass, we journey as one,
Facing each challenge until it is done.
In the light of compassion, we stand side by side,
Together we ascend, with love as our guide.

The echoes of laughter, the whispers of prayer,
In the heart of the many, is hope everywhere.
From mountains to valleys, our voices resound,
Together we ascend, where grace can be found.

Through trials we cherish, through joy we unite,
In the warmth of our bond, we shine ever bright.
With humility's power, we seek and we serve,
Together we ascend, it's truth that we preserve.

As the heavens embrace us, we find our peace,
In the strength of our gathering, we find release.
A footprint of love, on the path we create,
Together we ascend, it's never too late.

In Brotherhood's Embrace

In the heart of the storm, we find our rest,
In brotherhood's embrace, we are truly blessed.
With kindness as shelter, we stand as a wall,
Together we rise, answering the call.

With hands intertwined, we weather the night,
In the shadows we gather, seeking the light.
For every burden, a shoulder we'll lend,
In brotherhood's embrace, we rise and we mend.

Through tales of old, our legacy flows,
In laughter and sorrow, our love only grows.
Each step taken forward, a bond deeply traced,
In brotherhood's embrace, our fears are erased.

In silence we listen, and in joy we sing,
In unity's dance, our spirits take wing.
With a heart full of honor, we venture ahead,
In brotherhood's embrace, all paths will be tread.

As the sun sets low, and the stars appear,
In the warmth of our circle, there's nothing to fear.
For in every heartbeat, together we face,
In brotherhood's embrace, we find our place.

The Light We Share

In the twilight hour, a glow ignites,
With the love we carry, we banish the nights.
Through whispers of hope, we spread our wings,
The light we share, oh, how brightly it sings.

In the garden of souls, we plant every seed,
With kindness and grace, we nourish each need.
As stars light the heavens, our spirits declare,
In the light we share, we banish despair.

As shadows may lengthen, and fears may arise,
Our unity sparkles like stars in the skies.
With hearts intertwined, we embrace the fair,
In the light we share, all burdens we bear.

Through laughter and tears, we weave our design,
In this sacred journey, your hand within mine.
In the silence we find, a courage laid bare,
In the light we share, love is our prayer.

So let us encircle, in friendship so true,
With each step we take, we create something new.
In the glow of our hearts, let us always care,
In the light we share, our spirits lay bare.

Unity's Grace

In moments dark, we find the light,
Together we stand, hearts shining bright.
Hand in hand, we walk this road,
With love as our guide, we share the load.

Through trials faced, we rise above,
In every challenge, we show our love.
Bound in spirit, we journey forth,
Embracing peace, we find our worth.

In whispered prayers, our souls align,
A tapestry woven, divine design.
Unity's grace, a sacred song,
Together in faith, we grow strong.

With open arms, we nurture hope,
In quiet trust, we learn to cope.
Each step we take, a sacred dance,
In faith entwined, we seize the chance.

In every heart, a spark ignites,
With love's embrace, we scale new heights.
Unity's grace, forever to bind,
In the warmth of love, we seek and find.

Harmony in Trials

In shadows deep, we hear the call,
With faith as our anchor, we will not fall.
Through storms we face, together we'll stand,
In every heart, the strength to withstand.

When burdens weigh, we lift each other,
In times of sorrow, we find a brother.
With kindness shared, we soften the blow,
In love's embrace, our spirits grow.

Though paths are rough, we'll find the way,
In unity's grip, we will not sway.
With hands held high, we seek the light,
In darkest hours, we shine so bright.

Through trials faced, our spirits soar,
In harmony's song, forever more.
With every tear, a strength reborn,
In faith we rise, each day a new dawn.

In shared belief, we overcome fears,
With love's own grace, we dry the tears.
Together we stand, in grace we dwell,
In harmony's arms, all will be well.

Bound by Faith

In every whisper, hope is found,
With gentle hearts, we stand our ground.
A sacred bond, unbreakable thread,
In faith we rise, where angels tread.

Through trials faced, we learn to trust,
In every challenge, a common gust.
Guided by grace, we find our way,
With open hearts, we choose to stay.

When darkness looms, we find the flame,
In faith's embrace, we rise, reclaim.
With souls entwined, we'll face the fire,
In unity's glow, we lift each other higher.

Through valleys deep, we journey on,
In every step, a cherished song.
Bound by faith, we stand as one,
In love's embrace, our battle won.

In sacred circles, we gather near,
With faithful hearts, we cast out fear.
Together we soar, on wings of grace,
Bound by faith, we find our place.

Rising as One

In the dawn's light, we rise anew,
With hearts united, we sing our truth.
Together in spirit, we seek the way,
In every moment, we choose to pray.

With voices joined, we lift our song,
In unity's hold, we all belong.
Through trials faced, we won't despair,
For in love's grace, we find our share.

Hand in hand, we walk this earth,
In every heartbeat, we find our worth.
With open arms, we gather near,
In mutual strength, we conquer fear.

In sacred bonds, we take a stand,
Empowered by love, we change the land.
Through faith and hope, we break the chains,
In harmony's rhythm, freedom reigns.

With every heartbeat, our spirits soar,
Rising as one, forevermore.
In love's embrace, we stand as stars,
Together shining, no matter how far.

Hands Together

In the stillness, we unite,
With hands together, bringing light.
In prayerful whispers, hope anew,
We gather strength, our spirits true.

Together we rise, stronger still,
In faith and love, we find our will.
Each act of kindness, a sacred thread,
In this tapestry, our hearts are wed.

With open palms, we share our grace,
In every soul, we see His face.
Together we walk, side by side,
In the embrace of love, we abide.

Through trials faced and burdens shared,
In every moment, we are cared.
With hands together, we shape our fate,
In harmony, we celebrate.

So let us stand, united loud,
In every whisper, be feeling proud.
For in this bond, we find our way,
Hands together, we choose to pray.

Hearts Together

In the morning light, we gather near,
With hearts together, casting fear.
In love's embrace, we break the mold,
With every heartbeat, truth unfolds.

Through laughter shared and tears unveiled,
In joy and sorrow, we have sailed.
With open hearts, we seek the grace,
In every challenge, we find our place.

Together we sing, our voices soar,
In purest harmony, we explore.
With compassion's touch, we heal the pain,
In unity, our spirits reign.

With hearts together, we share the light,
In darkest times, we shine so bright.
With every prayer, our souls entwine,
In sacred bonds, our hearts align.

So let us walk this path so true,
In loving kindness, all we do.
With hearts together, we'll always stand,
In faith and love, hand in hand.

The Light of Community

In the gathering dusk, we find our way,
The light of community guides each day.
Together we shine, our spirits blaze,
In every heart, there's a song of praise.

In laughter shared, we build our dreams,
In unity's glow, love brightly beams.
With open arms, we embrace the fight,
In every struggle, we find the light.

Through giving hands and tender care,
In bonds of grace, we rise, we share.
In every voice, a purpose shines,
Within this circle, hope defines.

Together we stand, no one alone,
In cherished hearts, we find our home.
The light of community, a flame so true,
In every shadow, it shines anew.

With gratitude, we gather strong,
In unison, we sing our song.
In the light of community, we define,
A tapestry woven, forever divine.

Chains of Bonding Grace

In quiet moments, we intertwine,
Chains of bonding grace, truly divine.
With every link, we build our trust,
In love's embrace, we rise from dust.

Through trials faced, our spirits soar,
In chains of grace, we find the core.
With hands uplifted, we break the chains,
In every freedom, compassion reigns.

Together we bear the weight we choose,
In unity's strength, there's nothing to lose.
With hearts aligned, we treasure the space,
In chains of bonding, we find our place.

In shared struggles, we grow more wise,
With every challenge, our spirits rise.
Chains of bonding grace, ever tight,
In love's embrace, we shine so bright.

So let us cherish these ties we weave,
In faith and love, we shall believe.
For in these chains, our spirits sing,
In bonds of grace, new hope takes wing.

In the Shadow of Each Other

In the shadow of each other, we stand,
With open hearts, we lend a hand.
In shared silence, we find our peace,
From doubts released, our worries cease.

Through whispered prayers, we find the way,
In faith's embrace, we choose to stay.
In every struggle, we lift the weight,
In love's reflection, we navigate.

Together we walk, side by side,
In the shadows deep, our fears subside.
With gentle words, we heal the strife,
In every bond, we share this life.

In moments dark, we spark the light,
In the shadow of each other, we ignite.
With every heartbeat, our spirits flow,
In love's embrace, together we grow.

So let us cherish this sacred trust,
In the shadow of each other, we must.
For in this bond, forever we share,
In hearts united, we find our prayer.

Whispers of Support

In the quiet hum of prayer,
Hearts gather, with hope laid bare.
Each whisper a soft embrace,
Lifting spirits in this space.

When shadows fall, we remain,
Sharing joy, sharing pain.
Beyond the words, love runs deep,
In sacred bonds, our souls keep.

Together we stand so tall,
In faith's light, we shall not fall.
Through trials, our voices rise,
A symphony of the wise.

With each challenge we face,
We find strength in this grace.
In whispers, a promise made,
Forever in light's cascade.

So let our hearts align,
In the sacred design.
With hands open to the need,
Together, we plant the seed.

Unity in Struggle

In the darkest of our night,
We gather strength, hearts alight.
In union, we find our song,
Together, we surely belong.

Each tear shed, a shared story,
In our pain, we find the glory.
Through the valley, hand in hand,
In struggle, together we stand.

Bound by love, our mission clear,
In the silence, we draw near.
Voices lifted, a mighty roar,
In unity, our spirits soar.

With faith rooted, we will rise,
Facing storms with hopeful eyes.
Through trials and tests of faith,
We're united, no room for wraith.

As we walk this path of light,
We share the burden, ease the fight.
In every step, we'll proclaim,
Together, we carry love's flame.

Hands Held in Faith

When we join our hands in prayer,
The burdens light, a love we share.
In faith, we lift our eyes high,
Trusting in the reasons why.

Each palm pressed, a spirit's bond,
A connection that goes beyond.
In silence, strength is found,
In unity, our joy unbound.

Through every doubt and every fear,
With hands held tight, we persevere.
A circle of grace, so divine,
In each moment, our hearts entwine.

Moving forward, hearts ablaze,
In faith's embrace, we find our ways.
With every heartbeat, we connect,
In the light, we all reflect.

So let us walk, hand in hand,
In this sacred, promised land.
With love as our guiding light,
Together, we embrace the night.

Rising Beneath One Sky

Underneath one vast expanse,
We rise together, a sacred dance.
In the sun's warm, golden light,
Hearts awaken, taking flight.

Each soul shines, a brilliant star,
No matter the distance, no matter how far.
In our hearts, a burning flame,
In this journey, we are the same.

Through the tempests, we will steer,
In every smile, feel the cheer.
With faith guiding our way,
Together we thrive every day.

As the moon casts its gentle glow,
In this unity, love will flow.
Rising higher, dreams ignite,
A constellation shining bright.

So let us soar, hearts in sync,
In this union, we shall not sink.
Beneath one sky, we will rise,
In hope's embrace, we touch the skies.

Seeds of Unity

In the garden of hope we sow,
Each seed a dream for love to grow.
With gentle hands, we share the light,
Together we rise, through darkest night.

In every heart, a story waits,
To bind our souls, to open gates.
With faith as roots, we stand as one,
In harmony, our work begun.

We nurture bonds with tender care,
As flowers bloom, we share the air.
United by grace, our spirits soar,
In the seeds of unity, we explore.

Through trials faced, we find our strength,
In fellowship, we go the length.
With whispered prayers, our purpose clear,
Together we fight, together we cheer.

As branches reach, a canopy,
A shelter vast, for you and me.
In the garden where love is free,
Seeds of unity, our destiny.

Echoes of Faithful Hearts

In quiet corners, whispers rise,
Echoes of faith beneath the skies.
Bound by the vow, we'll stand in grace,
Hearts aligned, in this sacred space.

In every tear, a lesson learned,
In every song, a flame that burned.
Together we walk, through shadows deep,
With faithful hearts, our promise to keep.

The path is long, but we find light,
In unity's grasp, we take our flight.
With arms outstretched, we gather near,
Echoes of love, forever clear.

In moments shared, our spirits glide,
Through storms and calm, we bide the tide.
With courage strong, we face the night,
Echoes of faithful hearts, our might.

Through trials faced, we carry on,
With every dawn, a new love drawn.
In harmony, we find our way,
Faithful hearts, forever stay.

The Blessing of Many Paths

In every step, a choice we take,
The blessing lies in roads we make.
Different journeys, but the same goal,
Connecting lives, and warming souls.

Through winding trails, our lessons found,
In every meeting, love abound.
Embrace the paths that lead us here,
In diversity, we hold each dear.

With open hearts, we learn and grow,
Through every trial, the truth we know.
The blessing of many paths we share,
In unity, we breathe the air.

From mountains high to valleys low,
Together we rise, together we flow.
In every heart, a sacred song,
The blessing of many paths, lifelong.

In spirit's dance, we find our grace,
With every turn, we see His face.
Embracing all, we stand as one,
The blessing of many paths begun.

Sunlight Through Our Trials

In shadows cast, we seek the light,
Sunlight through trials, a hopeful sight.
With every fear, we find our way,
In darkest hours, we choose to stay.

Through raging storms, our spirits clear,
In faith, we find the strength to cheer.
For every tear, a lesson learned,
In the warmth of love, our hearts discerned.

As rays of hope break through the gloom,
We gather strength, dispelling doom.
Each trial faced, a step to grace,
Sunlight shining on every face.

In fellowship, we raise our hands,
Together we walk, with steadfast plans.
Through every challenge, together we rise,
Sunlight provides, our hearts advise.

In faith and love, we find the way,
Embracing light, we seize the day.
Through every trial, we learn to thrive,
Sunlight guides us, forever alive.

Milton Keynes UK
Ingram Content Group UK Ltd.
UKHW020039271124
451585UK00012B/938